A TASTE OF TAGORE

A TASTE OF
TAGORE

poetry * prose * prayers

Rabindranath Tagore

Compiled by Meron Shapland

with a Foreword by Deepak Chopra

green books

Published in 2011
by Green Books
Dartington Space, Dartington Hall, Totnes, Devon TQ9 6EN
www.greenbooks.co.uk

ISBN 978 1 900322 93 5

Contents

Prayers

Songs

Acknowledgements

My deepest gratitude goes to my mother, who introduced me to fine literature.

My appreciation and thanks go to Deepak Chopra for writing the foreword; to Satish Kumar for providing guidance; to Peggy O'Hare for being an inspiration and a valued friend; to William Radice for invaluable assistance with the layouts of Tagore's work; to our *satsang* group, in particular Vasilis Kardasis and Andy Cooney; to my dear friend Roby Braun for creating the cover; to Jeremy Cama and Jo Crosta for their support; to John Elford, Amanda Cuthbert and all at Green Books who have given guidance and care. And to my friends, thank you.

Foreword

*Why Tagore is relevant for the future of spirituality
and of humanity*

Although Rabindranath Tagore grew up in Edwardian times, he is more relevant today than ever before. His contribution to our understanding of spirituality as a domain of human awareness that is universal is deeply needed to repair our wounded soul and heal our planet. Born in Bengal in 1861, Rabindranath Tagore published a little book called *Gitanjali* in 1912, which is still his best-known work. He won the Nobel Prize for Literature in 1913 – the first Asian to win the prize.

He also painted, composed music, lectured, founded schools and established a university. Showered with praise and fame, he became a saint in his homeland and wandered the world until his death in 1941. These are the bare facts of a great life. Yet the cosmic dimension of Tagore's mind and heart are what capture our attention in these verses. His voice is humble – he calls himself a "hollow reed carried over hill and dale", and God is the flutist playing endless songs through him. But this humble instrument seems to know God personally. He is intimate with the reality of love as a spiritual force.

Tagore wrote of life and love but also made us see death as part of the continuum of life. I can think of no more healing words than those of Tagore. "When I want to know the most intimate truths of the universe, I turn to Him." Tagore knew that the most profound subjects – love, truth, compassion, birth and death – were His. Many others have written about love and death, but no one has joined them together with the passion of Tagore. Turning Death into another face of his Lord, Tagore actually saw himself as Death's beloved. When he cries "Death, oh my death, whisper to me! For you alone have I kept watch day after day," you can hear a rare emotion, pure ecstasy, in his voice.

The cosmic dimension of Tagore's mind is what captures our attention. To be so deeply religious and yet to include the everyday feelings that we all have is his unique gift. For Tagore had no need to romanticise or gloss over any feelings: "Don't be ashamed of tears," he says. "The earth's tears keep her flowers blooming."

The first-time reader of Tagore will be enchanted by the emotion and the music of Tagore's work – it goes beyond logic or even ordinary poetry, for Tagore was also a spiritual teacher whose view of the world turns our everyday perspective upside down.

Tagore's poems touch the innocence that is ever-present in us. To realise that death is an illusion, you either have to be very sophisticated or very simple. Tagore was both.

Deepak Chopra, 2011

Introduction

The idea of compiling a book for an audience perhaps unfamiliar with the profound and graceful writings of Rabindranath Tagore came to me one February afternoon in 2010, at our Richmond *satsang*. Satish Kumar joined us to share with our group his idea of a Tagore Festival and to invite us to contribute.

I wanted Tagore the man, and the breadth, depth and beauty of his thinking on certain subjects, to be made known to the reader at the beginning of this book. I therefore invite you to sit with him and gain insight into his thoughts through these prose extracts, before moving on to his other writings.

In conferring the Nobel Prize on Tagore in 1913, the committee had passed over Tolstoy, Yeats and George Bernard Shaw. Nehru, when he first heard of Tagore's passing, was in a British jail in India at the time and simply stated: "Gandhi and Tagore . . . India's great men . . . they were supreme as human beings."

Over the years, Tagore's poetry and prayers have never been too far away. For me he has such inner depth; a passion and a seemingly profound personal relationship with his God. He writes about the ebb and flow of life with such beauty. Tragedy struck him so many times during a period of his life that he contemplated suicide, but he pushed through and I believe his writings grew even deeper through these experiences.

For me, the most important thing was his non-sectarianism. He came from a Hindu family but recognised Buddha as the greatest human being ever to have lived (in his words), he extolled the Sermon on the Mount and translated the poems of Kabir, the mystic seer of Islam. His description of his own Bengali family was of "a confluence of three cultures: Hindu, Mohammedan, and British".

We in the West have moved forward in the last 60 years towards the fulfilment of Tagore's desire to bring East and West ever closer, and, in this UNESCO Year of Tagore, may we all continue to walk along his path to a deeper understanding of all cultures and self. I believe that his voice is as relevant to us today as it ever was, and will continue to be so for all time.

Meron Shapland

PROSE

Thoughts on my Life

I had a deep sense, almost from infancy, of the beauty of nature, an intimate feeling of companionship with the trees and the clouds, and felt in tune with the musical touch of the seasons in the air. At the same time I had a peculiar susceptibility to human kindness. All these craved expression, and naturally I wanted to give them my own expression.

Some say that my poems do not spring from the heart of the national traditions; some complain that they are incomprehensible, others that they are unwholesome. In fact, I have never had complete acceptance from my own people, and that too has been a blessing; for nothing is so demoralizing as unqualified success.

No poet should borrow his medium ready-made from some shop of respectability. He should not only have his own seeds but prepare his own soil. Each poet has his own distinct medium of language – not because the whole language is of his own making but because his individual use of it, having life's magic touch, transforms it into a special vehicle of his own creation.

The races of man have poetry in their heart, and it is necessary for them to give, as far as is possible, a perfect expression to their sentiments. For this they must have a medium, moving and pliant, which can freshly become their very own, age after age. All great languages have undergone and are still undergoing changes. Those languages which resist the spirit of change are doomed and will never produce great harvests of thought and literature. When forms become fixed, the spirit either weakly accepts its imprisonment within them or rebels. All revolutions consist of the fight of the within against invasion by the without.

Revolution must come, and men must risk revilement and misunderstanding, especially from those who want to be comfortable, who put their faith in materialism and convention, and who belong truly to the dead past and not to modern times – the past that had its age in distant antiquity, when physical flesh and size predominated, and not the mind of man.

The impertinence of material things is extremely old. The revelation of spirit in man is truly modern: I am on its side, for I am modern.

In regard to music, I claim to be something of a musician myself. I have composed many songs which have defied the canons of respectable orthodoxy, and good people are disgusted at the impudence of a man who is audacious only because he is untrained. But I persist, and God forgives me because I do not know what I do. Possibly that is the best way of doing things in the sphere of art.

I have been asked to let you know something about my own view of religion. One of the reasons why I always feel reluctant to speak about this is that I have not come to my own religion through the portals of passive acceptance of a particular creed owing to some accident of birth. I was born to a family who were pioneers in the revival in our country of a great religion, based upon the utterance of Indian sages in the Upanishads. But, owing to my idiosyncrasy of temperament, it was impossible for me to accept any religious teaching on the only ground that people in my surroundings believed it to be true. I could not persuade myself to imagine that I had a religion simply because everybody whom I might trust believed in its value.

Thus my mind was brought up in an atmosphere of freedom, freedom from the dominance of any creed that had its sanction in the definite authority of some scripture or in the teaching of some organized body of worshippers.

My religion essentially is a poet's religion. Its touch comes to me through the same unseen and trackless channels as does the inspiration of my music. My religious life has followed the same mysterious line of growth as has my poetical life. Somehow they are wedded to each other, and though their betrothal had a long period of ceremony, it was kept secret from me. Then suddenly came a day when their union was revealed to me.

God does not care to keep exposed the record of His power written in geological inscriptions, but He is proudly glad of the expression of beauty which He spreads on the green grass, in the flowers, in the play of colours on the clouds, in the murmuring music of running water.

That which merely gives us information can be explained in terms of measurement, but that which gives us joy cannot be explained by the facts of a mere grouping of atoms and molecules. Somewhere in the arrangement of this world there seems to be a great concern about giving us delight, which shows that, in the universe, over and above the meaning of matter and force, there is a message conveyed through the magic touch of personality. This touch cannot be analysed, it can only be felt.

Is it merely because the rose is round and pink that it gives me more satisfaction than the gold which could buy me the necessities of life, or any number of slaves? You may, at the outset, deny the truth that a rose gives more delight than a piece of gold. But you must remember that I am not speaking of artificial values. If we had to cross a desert whose sand was made of gold, then the cruel glitter of these dead particles would become a terror for us, and the sight of a rose would bring to us the music of paradise.

The final meaning of the delight which we find in a rose can never be in the roundness of its petals, just as the final meaning of the joy of music cannot be in a gramophone disk. Somehow we feel that through a rose the language of love reaches our heart. Do we not carry a rose to our beloved because in it is already embodied a message which, unlike our language of words, cannot be analysed? Through this gift of a rose we utilize a universal language of joy for our own purposes of expression.

Mere information of facts, mere discovery of power, belongs to the outside and not to the inner soul of things. Gladness is the one criterion of truth, and we know when we have touched Truth by the music it gives, by the joy of the greeting it sends forth to the truth in us. It is not as ether waves that we receive our light; the morning does not wait for some scientist for its introduction to us. In the same way, we touch the infinite reality immediately within us only when we receive the pure truth of love or goodness, not through the explanation of theologians, not through the erudite discussion of ethical doctrines.

In the night we stumble over things and become acutely conscious of their individual separateness, but the day reveals the great unity which embraces them. And the man, whose inner vision is bathed in an illumination of his consciousness, at once realises the spiritual unity reigning supreme over all differences of race, and his mind no longer awkwardly stumbles over individual facts of separateness in the human world, accepting them as final; he realises that peace is in the inner harmony which dwells in truth, and not in any outer adjustments; that beauty carries an eternal assurance of our spiritual relationship to reality, which waits for its perfection in the response of our love.

Thoughts on Education

For us to maintain the self-respect which we owe to ourselves and to our creator, we must make the purpose of our education nothing short of the highest purpose of man, the fullest growth and freedom of soul. It is pitiful to have to scramble for small pittances of fortune. Only let us have access to the life that goes beyond death and rises above all circumstances, let us find our God, let us live for that ultimate truth which emancipates us from the bondage of the dust and gives us the wealth, not of things but of inner light; not of power but of love. Such emancipation of soul we have witnessed in our country among men devoid of book-learning and living in absolute poverty. In India we have the inheritance of this treasure of spiritual wisdom. Let the object of our education be to open it out before us and to give us the power to make the true use of it in our life, and offer it to the rest of the world when the time comes, as our contribution to its eternal welfare.

It will be difficult for others than Indians to realise all the associations that are grouped round the word ashram, the forest sanctuary. For it blossomed in India like its own lotus, under a sky generous in its sunlight and starry splendour. India's climate has brought to us the invitation of the open air; the language of her mighty rivers is solemn in their chants; the limitless expanse of her plains encircles our homes with the silence of the world beyond; there the sun rises from the marge of the green earth like an offering of the unseen to the altar of the Unknown, and it goes down to the west at the end of the day like a gorgeous ceremony of nature's salutation to the Eternal. In India the shades of the trees are hospitable, the dust of the earth stretches its brown arms to us, the air with its embraces clothes us with warmth. These are the unchanging facts that ever carry their suggestions to our minds, and therefore we feel it is India's mission to realise the truth of the human soul in the Supreme Soul through its union with the soul of the world. This mission had taken its natural form in the forest schools in the ancient time. And it still urges us to seek for the vision of the infinite in all forms of creation, in the human relationships of love; to feel it in the air we breathe, in the light in which we open our eyes, in the water in which we bathe, in the earth on which we live and die. Therefore I know – and I know it from my own experience – that the students and the teachers who have come together in this ashram are daily growing towards the emancipation of their minds into the consciousness of the infinite, not through any process of teaching or outer discipline but by the help of an unseen atmosphere of aspiration that surrounds the place and the memory of a devoted soul who lived here in intimate communion with God.

At any rate during the early period of education children should come to their lesson of truths through natural processes – directly through persons and things.

Naturally the soles of our feet are so made that they become the best instruments for us to stand upon the earth and to walk with. From the day we commenced to wear shoes we minimized the purpose of our feet. With the lessening of their responsibility they have lost their dignity, and now they lend themselves to be pampered with socks, slippers and shoes of all prices and shapes and misproportions. For us it amounts to a grievance against God for not giving us hooves instead of beautifully sensitive soles. But I have no hesitation in asserting that the soles of children's feet should not be deprived of their education, provided for them by nature, free of cost. Of all the limbs we have they are the best adapted for intimately knowing the earth by their touch. For the earth has her subtle modulations of contour which she only offers for the kiss of her true lovers – the feet.

I believe that the object of education is the freedom of mind which can only be achieved through the path of freedom – though freedom has its risk and responsibility as life itself has. I know it for certain, though most people seem to have forgotten it, that children are living beings – more living than grown-up people, who have built their shells of habit around them. Therefore it is absolutely necessary for their mental health and development that they should not have mere schools for their lessons, but a world whose guiding spirit is personal love. It must be an ashram where men have gathered for the highest end of life, in the peace of nature; where life is not merely meditative, but fully awake in its activities; where boys' minds are not being perpetually drilled into believing that the ideal of the self-idolatry of the nation is the truest ideal for them to accept; where they are bidden to realise man's world as God's Kingdom, to whose citizenship they have to aspire; where the sunrise and sunset and the silent glory of stars are not daily ignored; where nature's festivities of flowers and fruit have their joyous recognition from man; and where the young and the old, the teacher and the student, sit at the same table to partake of their daily food and the food of their eternal life.

Thoughts on Art

The principal object of art, also, being the expression of personality, and not of that which is abstract and analytical, it necessarily uses the language of picture and music. This has led to a confusion in our thought that the object of art is the production of beauty; whereas beauty in art has been the mere instrument and not its complete and ultimate significance.

As a consequence of this, we have often heard it argued whether manner, rather than matter, is the essential element in art. Such arguments become endless, like pouring water into a vessel whose bottom has been taken away. These discussions owe their origin to the idea that beauty is the object of art, and, because mere matter cannot have the property of beauty, it becomes a question whether manner is not the principal factor in art.

But the truth is, analytical treatment will not help us in discovering what is the vital point in art. For the true principle of art is the principle of unity. When we want to know the food-value of certain of our diets, we find it in their component parts; but its taste-value is in its unity, which cannot be analysed. Matter, taken by itself, is an abstraction which can be dealt with by science; while manner, which is merely manner, is an abstraction which comes under the laws of rhetoric. But when they are indissolubly one, then they find their harmonics in our personality, which is an organic complex of matter and manner, thoughts and things, motive and actions.

Therefore we find all abstract ideas are out of place in true art, where, in order to gain admission, they must come under the disguise of personification. This is the reason why poetry tries to select words that have vital qualities – words that are not for mere information, but have become naturalised in our hearts and have not been worn out of their shapes by too constant use in the market. For instance, the English word 'consciousness' has not yet outgrown the cocoon stage of its scholastic inertia, therefore it is seldom used in poetry; whereas its Indian synonym 'chetana' is a vital word and is of constant poetical use. On the other hand, the English word 'feeling' is fluid with life, but its Bengali synonym 'anubhuti' is refused in poetry, because it merely has a meaning and no flavour. And likewise there are some truths, coming from science and philosophy, which have acquired life's colour and taste, and some which have not. Until they have done this, they are, for art, like uncooked vegetables, unfit to be served at a feast.

For man, as well as for animals, it is necessary to give expression to feelings of pleasure and displeasure, fear, anger and love. In animals, these emotional expressions have gone little beyond their bounds of usefulness. But in man, though they still have roots in their original purposes, they have spread their branches far and wide in the infinite sky high above their soil. Man has a fund of emotional energy which is not all occupied with his self-preservation. This surplus seeks its outlet in the creation of Art, for man's civilization is built upon his surplus.

How utility and sentiment take different lines in their expression can be seen in the dress of a man compared with that of a woman. A man's dress, as a rule, shuns all that is unnecessary and merely decorative. But a woman has naturally selected the decorative, not only in her dress, but in her manners. She has to be picturesque and musical to make manifest what she truly is, because, in her position in the world, woman is more concrete and personal than man. She is not to be judged merely by her usefulness, but by her delightfulness. Therefore she takes infinite care in expressing, not her profession, but her personality.

Thoughts on Construction
versus Creation

Construction is for a purpose, it expresses our wants; but creation is for itself, it expresses our very being. We make a vessel because water has to be fetched. It must answer the question why. But when we take infinite trouble to give it a beautiful form, no reason has to be assigned. It is something which is ultimate; it is for the realisation of our own spirit which is free, which is glad. If, in the works of our life, needs make themselves too domineering, purposes too obtrusive, if something of our complete humanity is not expressed at the same time, then these works become ugly and unspiritual.

In love, in goodness, man himself is revealed; these express no want in him; they show the fullness of his nature which flows out of himself and therefore they are purely creative. They are ultimate – therefore, in our judgement of man's civilization, they give us the true criterion of perfection.

Creation is the revelation of truth through the rhythm of forms. It has a dualism consisting of the expression and the material. Of these two wedded companions the material must keep in the background and continually offer itself as a sacrifice to its absolute loyalty to the expression. And this is true of all things, whether in our individual life or in our society.

When the material makes itself too aggressive and furiously multiples itself into unmeaning voluminousness, then the harmony of creation is disturbed and truth is obscured. If the lamp takes a perverse pride in displaying its oil, then the light remains unrevealed. The material must know that it has no idea of completeness in itself, that it must not hold our temptations to decoy men under its destination away from their creative activities.

We see a flower, but not matter. Matter in a laboratory has its use but no expression. This expression alone is creation; it is an end in itself. So also does our civilization find its completeness when it expresses humanity, not when it displays its power to amass materials.

When humanity lacks this music of soul, then society becomes a mechanical arrangement of compartments, of political and social classifications. Such a machine is a mere aping of creation, and not having unity at its heart it enforces it in its outer structure for mere convenience. In it the life that grows and feels is hurt, and either is crushed into insensibility or breaks out in constant convulsions.

The vital harmony is lacking today in unity of man, for the formalness of law and regulation has displaced the living ideal of personality from human affairs, and science has taken the office of religion in man's greatest creative work, his civilization.

The diversion of man's energy to the outside is producing an enormous quantity of materials which may give rise in us to the pride of power but not the joy of life. The hugeness of things is every day overawing the greatness of man, and the gap between matter and life is growing wider. For when things become too many, they refuse to be completely assimilated to life, thus becoming its most dangerous rival, as is an excessively large pile of fuel to the fire.

*

Growth there must be in life. But growth does not mean an enlargement through additions. Things, such as masonry-structure, which have to be constructed by a gradual building up of materials, do not show their perfection until they are completed. But living things start with their wholeness from the beginning of their growth. Life is a continual process of synthesis. A child is complete in itself; it does not wait for the perfection of its lovability till it has come to the end of its childhood. The enjoyment of a song begins from the beginning of the singing and continually follows its course to the end. But the man whose sole concern is the acquisition of power or material deals with a task which is cursed with eternal incompleteness. For things find no meaning in themselves when their magnitude consists solely of accumulated bulk. They acquire truth only when they are assimilated to a living idea. This assimilation becomes impossible so long as the passion for acquisition occupies all our mind, when there is no large leisure for life force to pursue its own great work of self-creation.

*

But in recent centuries has come a devastating change in our mentality with regard to the acquisition of money. We not only pursue it but bend our knees to it. For us its call has become the loudest of all voices, reaching even the sanctuaries of our temples. That it should be allowed a sufficiently large place in society there can be no question, but it becomes an outrage when it occupies those seats which are specially reserved for the immortals, by bribing us, by tampering with our moral pride, by recruiting the best strength of society on its side in a traitor's campaign against human ideals, disguising with the help of pageantry and pomp its innate insignificance.

Thoughts on International Relations

All great civilizations are built upon numberless ruins – the topped-down towers of victory and wealth. It is only human beings in this world of life who have found their greatness through the desperate urgings of unfavourable circumstances. Humanity has never been pampered, petted and spoilt by Nature, but rather respected by being given constant opportunity to overcome the obstacles of failures and losses.

You will realise that the people's life, like a waterfall, finds its full force of movement through courageous leaps from peak to peak of new trials.

The nature of the people depends for its manifestation upon its creative personality. It has religion, arts, literature, traditions of social responsibility and co-operation. Its wealth to maintain itself and power of defence are secondary; they are not the ultimate ends for the people. But the Nation manifests itself in its property.

The people represent life, the nation materials; when they are in harmony, that is to say, when material possessions keep to their own limits and the creative life is unhampered in its spontaneous activity, then civilization is hospitable and generous.

But when material possessions become too vast for a people, or when in competition with others the desire for material wealth rouses its ambition, then all its time and mind are occupied with very little else. The man who is a 'millionaire' is dragged by the very weight of his millions to the path of the multitude of millions. Then he has no time for culture, or for the poetry of life; he strictly barricades himself against visitors, whom he cannot but suspect to be self-seekers, being selfish in his own outlook upon life. In other words he becomes professional, and the human in him is banished into the shade.

Since Nature's storehouse of power and wealth has been opened by the help of science, some people who know how to take advantage of it have suddenly grown enormously rich and others are incited to follow their example. The people who were human, who were creative and social in their self-expression, have become professional, enormously self-centred and anti-social in their tendency of mind. Material wealth and power, with their very bulk, have occupied the greater part of the space, time and mind of the people, necessitating a tremendous expense of thought and resources for ensuring their safety.

Material possessions create the worse division in human society when they are disproportionately big and naturally unmindful of moral responsibility. Therefore the Nation, the presiding genius of the material department of the people, cannot but be hard and exclusive. And in the modern age this department has become the most proudly domineering of all other manifestations of human society. It has made the craving for money universal and has given the name of Progress to the raising of the material standard of living.

In the East, we have had the courage to have faith even in impossible ideals. You all know that it was a prophet of the East who could say, 'Love your enemies.' You know, too, of another prophet of the East who could say, 'Conquer anger by non-anger and evil by goodness.' There are those in the West who have accepted these teachings in their churches and yet who feel extremely nervous when they are reminded of them, when they find that such teaching is commercially unprofitable and politically inconvenient.

A Prophet has arisen in India, who has likewise proclaimed that you have to conquer violence by non-violence. He speaks like a prophet of the East and insists that what has been translated into the Bible of the West must not only be pursued in the personal lives of individuals but must be given the best possible expression in our national lives.

Great tribulations in our history should never fail to give us the occasion to bring out the best resources of our life, so as not only to reveal them to the outer world, but – and this is more valuable – to reveal them to ourselves. If today you can discover some hidden source of magnanimity with which to face the insult and injury, if you can keep the majesty of your mind unimpaired, then you will be happy, and future generations will be thankful to you.

The Kingdom of Heaven is here on this earth. It is there, where we realise our best relations with our fellow-beings, where there is no mutual suspicion and misunderstanding – there is the Kingdom of Heaven, in the spirit of comradeship and love. Christ was right when He said that the path to such a Kingdom is closed for him who thinks more of his money than of his soul, more of his personal right than of his human responsibility. Now that the whole human world has surrendered itself to the lure of money and power, the severance of human relationship is everywhere becoming evident and the fight between classes is spreading wide.

Let me appeal to your imagination. If we could go back into the distant past, we would know that groups of men grew into great peoples through overcoming a feeling of distrust and cultivating sympathy for each other. It was not at all easy; for our passions are individualistic, our selfishness immensely strong. And yet the impossible has been attained in some societies. A system of discipline has been established, the sentiments of sympathy cultivated, and the ferocious savage has been tamed on a wholesale scale. We must also know that those who went on indulging in their selfish isolation perished.

In the early history of life in this world, with its display of stupendous bodily bulk and strength, when puny man first appeared on this earth, could his final victory have been predicated by the logic of appearance? In the same manner, it is apparently unbelievable today that only those who can overcome the egoistic sense of nationalism, who can develop the understanding of sympathy that pierces through barriers of race differences, who have the enduring strength of meekness, will inherit the earth; and not those who are imagined to be born rulers of men.

*

Hold up to us something which is your very own and not mere imitation. Do you not see how this malady of imitation is rapidly spreading from shore to shore, from nation to nation? It has the same monotony of features, in its offices, barracks, dress and manners, its attitude of mind. Every people in this world is vying with its neighbour to copy it, because being non-living it is easy to copy indefinitely. It is a mask that can be precisely similar in its multiplication, not a face which has spontaneous variety of self-expression.

But the mask can easily smother the living individuality of the face. That is what is happening everywhere in the world – the monotony of the nation killing the individuality of the people. The stone pavement, which can be made in the same stereotyped plan everywhere, deprives the soil of its unique personality of flowers and harvest. Through this deadening influence even your arts and crafts, all the delicate idioms of expression in your life and surroundings, are fast losing their own living character and stiffening into the standardised convention made in a foreign world. The Nation makes this mould, which may be useful; but we cannot afford to pay its cost with the inspiration of creative life, which is inherent in living peoples.

Whenever the spirit of the Nation has come it has destroyed sympathy and beauty, and driven out the generous obligations of human relationship from the hearts of men. It has spread the ugliness of its cities and its markets into the minds and enthroned the demon of deformity in the hearts of men. Though today it dominates the spirit of man everywhere in the world, it will die like the worm which lies in the heart of the fruit that it has devoured. It will die; but unfortunately it may meanwhile destroy things of unrivalled worth, the products of centuries of self-control and spiritual training.

POEMS

Life

This world is beautiful. I do not want to die.
I wish to live in the life of man,
and have a place in his living heart,
as in a sunbright flowerful garden.
Oh, the ceaseless ripple of life on earth,
the meetings and partings so happy and sad!
With human joys and griefs I shall wreathe my
    song,
and live for ever in the deathless life of man.
If I fail, then may I have
a little place in your midst, my friends,
and make new songs at morn and eve,
like flowers that bloom to be culled by you.
Pick my flowers with a smile on your face,
and throw them away when they fade.

New Birth

New deliverer –
    the new age eagerly looks
        to the path of your coming.
What message have you brought
  to the world? In the mortal arena
What seat has been prepared for you?
    What new form of address
  have you brought to be used
in the worship of God in Man? What song of heaven
  have you heard before coming?
  What great weapon for the fighting of evil
have you placed in the quiver, bound to the waist
    of the young warrior?
Will you, perhaps, where a tide of blood besmirches your path,
  where there is malice and discord,
    construct a dam of peace,
  a place of meeting and pilgrimage?
Who can say if there is written on your forehead
  the invisible mark
  of the triumph of some great striving?
Today we search for your unwritten name:
  you seem to be just off the stage,
  like an imminent star of morning.
  Infants bring again and again
  a message of reassurance –
they seem to promise deliverance, light, dawn.

Not my Achievement

It's not my achievement that I trust. I know the constant waves of time will break upon it day by day and obliterate it.

My faith is in myself; this cup I have filled with the universe and drunk. And filled it too with every moment's love.

The weight of sorrow made no crack, its art was blackened by no dust.

When I finally leave the stage, I know the flowering grove will season after season bear witness that I loved this world.

A lifetime's gift, this love is the truth. At the time of my departure this truth, unfading, will deny death.

On my Birthday

As I step into the eightieth year of my life, my mind wakes to this wonder today:

In the silent flood of light of the fiery stream of a billion stars that sweep at unimaginable speed through the soundless void, I have suddenly arisen in the linked history of centuries like an instant's spark in the festival of eternal creation underneath that sky, dark and limitless.

I have come to a world where aeon after aeon life's plasma rose from the womb of the sea and revealed its secret and splendid identity as it spread its branches in many a changing guise in the immense abyss of matter.

The drowsy shadows of an imperfect twilight existence had brooded over the animal world for ages, waiting anxiously-for whom?

At the end of countless days and nights man appeared on the stage of life with slow heavy steps. New lamps were lit one after the other, new values found form and voice; in an ethereal glow man saw the image of his splendid future.

On the world's stage is seen in act after act the slow unfolding of consciousness.

I too have dressed for my part among the actors in the drama. To my delighted wonder, I too have been called to discover the stage.

This world of life, this earthly dwelling of the soul with its sky and light and wind, its earth, sea and mountain hides a deep purpose and wheels round the sun.

Bound to that mystery, I came eighty years ago and shall depart in a few years time.

The Introduction

Once my boat, moved by the fresh winds of early spring, stopped at this landing place. You had all crowded round and asked, 'Who are you and where do you go?'

The river swelled, the boat tugged at the ropes. I sat alone and sang about the pangs of youth. Young lovers beneath flowering trees heard my song, plucked the Ashoka bloom and offered it as a gift, saying, 'He is one of us.' This alone was my first introduction.

The flood tide ended, the waves no longer rippled and laughed. The languid song of the cuckoo suddenly brought back to mind the memory of forgotten days. The golden champak drooped and was carried far away. Torn shreds from the gay invitation of festival nights in early spring, they were now meaningless.

The ebb-tide strongly pulled the boat towards the far-off sea. Boys and girls, young travellers of a new age, looked at me from a distance and asked, 'Who is it that sails in his boat towards the setting sun?'

I tuned my harp and sang once again, 'Let my only description be that I am one of you. Let this and nothing else be my final introduction.'

The Impermanence

A traveller am I on the roads of the world. In my wanderings have I seen lands famed in story and shorn of all glory today. I have seen the unheeded ruins of insolent might – its banner of victory is gone with the wind, like boisterous laughter stilled into silence by a sudden thunder-clap.

I have found stupendous pride humbled to the dust, dust on which the beggar spreads his tattered rags, dust on which the traveller leaves the print of weary steps to be effaced by the ceaseless march of unnumbered feet.

I have seen a world long dead lie entombed in layer below layer of sand like some stately ship struck by a sudden storm and sunk in a leaden sea with its cargo of hopes and songs and memories.

Among such symbols of impermanence I move, and feel in the very throbbing of my heart the utter stillness of the infinite.

Vitality

The vitality that flows in waves night and day through every vein of my body, flows out to conquer the universe; pulsates through the world in amazing rhythm and cadence; inspires every pore of the earth's soil with the thrill of a million grass-blades growing; blossoms into flowers and young leaves; sways, year after year, in the ceaseless ebb and flow of the undulating world-wide sea of life and death. That endless vitality, absorbed into my being, exalts me in every limb. In my veins dances today that vast rhythm of aeons.

Recovery – 14[*]

Every day in the early morning this faithful dog
sits quietly beside my chair
for as long as I do not acknowledge his presence
by the touch of my hand.
The moment he receives this small recognition,
waves of happiness leap through his body.
In the inarticulate animal world
only this creature
has pierced through good and bad and seen
complete man,
has seen him for whom
life may be joyfully given,
that object of a free outpouring of love
whose consciousness points the way
to the realm of infinite consciousness.
When I see that dumb heart
revealing its own humility
through total self-surrender,
I feel unequal to the worth
his simple perception has found in the nature of man.
The wistful anxiety in his mute gaze
understands something he cannot explain:
it directs me to the true meaning of man in the universe.

* Untitled poem no. 14 from the volume *Recovery*.

Sister

West-country labourers are digging up earth for a kiln by the river.

The young daughter of one of them comes daily to the ghat to scour pots and pans. She comes running, her brass bracelets tinkling on the brass utensils. She is very busy, almost bent under the weight of work, all day.

Her little brother, shaven, muddy and naked, follows her like a tame animal; sits down on the high bank as she tells him, and waits with quiet patience for her work to be over.

She leaves for home with a full pitcher on her head, plates on her left hip, and her brother's hand in her right hand. The sister, herself a child is also a mother in their mother's absence.

Question

God, again and again through the ages you have sent messengers
            to this pitiless world:
They have said, 'Forgive everyone', they have said 'Love one
                                        another –
        rid our hearts of evil.'
They are revered and remembered, yet still in these dark days
we turn them away with hollow greetings, from outside the
                                        doors of our houses.

And meanwhile I see secretive hatred murdering the helpless
            under cover of night;
And Justice weeping silently and furtively at power misused,
            no hope of redress.
I see young men working themselves into a frenzy,
in agony dashing their heads against stone to no avail.

My voice is choked today; I have no music in my flute:
            black moonless night
has imprisoned my world, plunged it into nightmare. And this
            is why, with tears in my eyes, I ask:
Those who have poisoned your air, those who have extinguished
                                        your light,
Can it be that you have forgiven them? Can it be that you love
                                        them?

Deliverance

Salvation in a hermit's cave?
No, not for me.

I shall retain a thousand ties and in their midst savour the bliss of liberation.

I shall take this world, this jar of clay, and fill it again and again with your nectar that has many flavours and colours.

I shall light the lamp of my universe, and with its million wicks illumine your temple.

I shall not shut the doors of my senses – no, never. The joy of song, and sight, and fragrance, – I shall keep them all and through them gain the joy of meeting you.

Then shall my craving burn itself out in freedom and my love find its fulfilment in devotion.

The Riddle

The one she loves – she loves to make him weep. Each time a new enigma, she confounds the image in his heart. Her light now shade, her shade now light, contrives his constant doubt. With great pretence of wounded pride she has him on his knees. Like autumn's magic showers from harmless-looking clouds, her glance suggests encouragement, but lightning shoots behind.

Why with disconcerting laughter scatter a lover's pleas? Then fall herself a victim of the cruel game? With grieving heart to get back whom she has turned away, she shatters into pieces her own wounded vanity. Why in the sky of her mind all day this wild madly sporting wind? To want to go one way and yet go the other, who can understand? Not she!

Deep in her mind, unknown to herself, what conflict with herself? Her anger is against herself and so she hurts another. But suddenly with molten pity she is at his feet, pouring out her heart and mind. Is her name, Heyali*?

* The nearest English equivalent meaning is 'riddle'.

Infinite Love

It seems it's you I have loved in a hundred
        forms, unending:
birth after birth, through the ages.
In many a form you have taken and swung
        around your neck the garland of songs my
        heart has stitched in sweet enchantment;
birth after birth, through the ages.

As I listen to that old-time song of pain and
        primeval love-
the old, old tale of meeting and parting-
and as I gaze into the infinite past,
at last though the darkness of Time appears
        your form like the pole-star with memories
        eternally laden.

From the heart of Time without beginning,
        we two have floated down in a double
        stream of passion.
We two have lived in a million lovers,
in the bashful smile of kissing and the tears of
        long partition,
tasting the same old love in forms for ever new.

And now that love of all the ages has met its
     last fulfilment in a heaped up offering at
     your feet.
In you are all the joys and anguish and all
     affections of the heart.
In a single love are blended the memories of
     all other passions,
and all the songs that poets have sung through
     the ages.

The Look

I wonder if your eyes learnt their twilight
    spell from the evening itself!
When you look at me, the shades of twilight
    descend on my heart and stars begin to
    shine.
Who could have guessed that such riches
    were hid in the recesses of my heart?
Now through your eyes I have seen my own
    heart.

You never sing and yet your silence teaches
    me songs: You bind my soul to the dreamy
    tranquil music of *Purabi*.

In tune with its melody I sing in loneliness
    gazing at the sky.
And the tunes reach the darkness and are lost
    in eternity!

First Kiss

The skies lowered their eyes and grew silent.
The birds ceased to sing.
The wind dropped, rippling waters stilled at
    once and forest murmurs faded in the heart
    of the forest.
The horizon came down on the silent earth
    along the lonely bank of the silent river in
    the still shadow of the evening.
At that instant, at the solitary silent window
    we kissed each other for the first time.
All at once evening bells rang out in the
    temple and filled the sky.
The eternal stars shivered and our eyes filled
    with tears.

Two Women

At the churning of primeval seas at the hour
       of creation, there arose two women from
       the unplumbed sea-bed;
Urvashi, the beautiful, the queen of desire, the
       dancer of heaven;

The One disrupts the ascetic's meditation, and
       with loud laughter steals his heart and soul,
serving him with fire-filled tankards of Spring-
       time wine, scattering with both hands the
       flowery delirium of Spring;
passion-red roses and unslumbering songs of youth.

The other laves you with dewy tears and turns
       you back to tender yearnings,
to the fullness of the golden peace of fruit-
       laden autumn;
brings you back to the blessings of the
       universe, to the sweet serene smile of
       unwavering grace;
gently brings you back to the sacred
       confluence of life and death,
       to the temple of the infinite.

The Prisoner

Take those fettering arms away,
stop those kisses like draughts of wine.
Close and stuffy is this flowery prison;
my captive heart set free, my love.
This night of full moon endless seems,
I pine for light of dawn in the sky.
Caught in meshes of your long loose hair,
from you shall I ever escape?
Your eager fingers, meeting together,
are weaving all over me a tactile net.
Whenever I open my drowsy eyes,
I see that moon with its non-stop smile.

    Take my fetters off, set me free:
    My free heart then I'll lay at your feet.

Alone

Sleep thou tonight, I shall sit watching by thy door and keep the light burning.

So long thou didst love, from now on I shall have to love thee in loneliness.

Thou will never again adorn thyself for my sake, but I shall through long days and nights deck my heart with flowers for thee.

Oblivious of fatigue and pain, thy arms have till now served me tirelessly but today I shall relieve them of all work and place them on my brow.

Thou hast offered thy mind and body and today thy worship done, thou departest from me, but from today my homage of tears and hymns of adoration shall be for thee alone.

The End

When the lights on the stage went out one by one, and the theatre was emptied of audience, my mind sank to quiet at the beckoning of silence, like a sleep whose dream-pictures are inked out in the darkness.

The make-up that I had fashioned so long for my stage-appearance since the curtain went up, came to nothing in a moment.

To present myself to the multitude I had decked myself in a variety of colours and insignia: all these were wiped out.

The depth of my fullness in myself reduced me to a wondering silence like that of the clear sky hushed in star-lit self-realisation when the variegated make-up of the earth fades into the blank of the day's end that witnesses the funeral of the sun.

The Beacon

There is a lone girl on the darkening beach who looks at the sky and floats her lighted lamp on the water.

She knows that her mother has gone to heaven and is hopeful that she will return by the ferry provided by the lamp.

The world swarms with millions, the roads that cross the earth are numberless, many are the countries that remain unknown and strange mountains raise their heads: in the midst of this multiplicity can the mother see from heaven the tiny nook where the two of them-brother and sister-live?

Does their mother go seeking for them in the darkness and lose her way again and again among the clustered stars in the infinite void?

The daughter's hand has lit a lamp and will keep it burning so that the mother may recognise the light from across the far off spaces.

In their sleep, will the mother come to their motherless bed and kiss them goodnight night after night?

The Final Offering

At the far end of the stage of the world's play I stand. Each moment do I see the shore beyond the darkness where in the vast consciousness of the Unmanifest I once lay merged.

On this morning spring to my mind the words of the seer, 'Lift, lift thy veil of light, O Sun, that in thy inmost core of radiance I may behold my own true Self.'

The 'I' whose breath of life at the end of day is one with the air, whose body ends in ashes-may that 'I' not cast its shadow on the path disguised as Truth.

In the playhouse of the world, many a time and oft have I tasted immortality in sorrow and in joy. Again and again have I seen the Infinite through the veil of the limited. For me the final meaning of life lay there: In beauty's forms, in harmonies divine.

Today, when the door of the playhouse opens I shall make my final bow, and leave behind in the temple of the earth my offerings of a life-time that no death can touch.

Farewell

It is time for the bird to leave. Soon the forest winds shall scatter to the ground the nest bereft, shaken and songless.

With the dried leaves and flowers, I shall be swept away at the day's end to the pathless wastes of space beyond the setting sun.

For ages this friendly earth has been my home. I have heard the call of spring full of gracious gifts and sweet with mango buds. The *Ashoka* blooms have yearned for my songs and I have filled them with my love. Sometime *Vaisakh* storms have raged, the warm dust has choked my voice and crippled my wings.

Blessed am I in all this. Life's honour has been mine.

When my tired journey here will be over, I shall look back once and leave an humble salute as my last homage to the Lord of Life.

The Borderland – 9[*]

I saw, in the twilight of flagging consciousness,
my body floating down an ink-black stream
with its mass of feelings, with its varied emotion,
with its many-coloured life-long store of memories,
with its flutesong. And as it drifted on and on
its outlines dimmed; and among familiar tree-shaded
villages on the banks, the sounds of evening
worship grew faint, doors were closed, lamps
were covered, boats were moored to the ghats. Crossings
from either side of the stream stopped; night thickened;
from the forest-branches fading birdsong offered
self-sacrifice to a huge silence.
dark formlessness settled over all diversity
of land and water. As shadow, as particles, my body
fused with endless night. I came to rest
at the altar of the stars. Alone, amazed, I stared
upwards with hands clasped and said: 'Sun, you have removed
your rays: show now your loveliest, kindliest form
that I may see the Person who dwells in me as in you.'

[*] Untitled poem no. 9 from the volume *The Borderland*.

A Hundred Years from Today / 1996*

Who are you reading curiously this poem
    of mine
a hundred years from now?
Shall I be able to send to you
    –steeped in the love of my heart–
the faintest touch of this spring morning's joy,
the scent of a flower,
a bird-song's note,
a spark of today's blaze of colour
a hundred years from now?

Yet, for once, open your window on the south
and from your balcony
gaze at the far horizon.
Then, sinking deep in fancy
think of the floating down
from some far heaven of bliss
to touch the heart of the world
a hundred years ago;
think of the young spring day
wild, impetuous and free;
and of the south wind
–fragrant with the pollen of flowers–
rushing on restless wings to paint the earth
with the radiant hues of youth
a hundred years before your day.

And think, how his heart aflame,
his whole being rapt in song,
a poet was awake that day
to unfold like flowers
his myriad thoughts
with what wealth of love!-
one morning a hundred years ago.

A hundred years from now
who is the new poet singing his songs to you?
Across the years I send him
the joyous greeting of this spring.
May my song echo for a while,
on your spring day,
in the beating of your heart,
in the murmur of bees,
in the rustling of leaves,-
a hundred years from today.

*This poem is known by both these names – it was written in 1896.

PRAYERS

O Make Me Thy Servant

O make me thy servant from today.
Give thy orders day and night, O Lord, amidst the mind.
Keep me engaged at thy service at the door of the
    universe.
Tear off all constraints of passion, all tempting expectation.
Drive, drive away fear from people.
Keep me devoted to goodness in silence and *sans*
    languor.
Drown me in the stream of joy.

The World Gone Mad

With hatred the world today has gone mad, adding a new conflict with each new dawn. Crooked are its paths, tangled are its bonds of greed. The world aches for Your new coming.

Come, O You of boundless life, embodiment of virtue and compassion with Your voice of eternal hope. Let the lotus of Your infinite love open its petals in Your light.

O Serene, O Free, in Your immeasurable mercy, wipe away all dark stains from the heart of this earth.

Come, O You, the giver of immortal gifts, teach us hard sacrifice. Let our pride be the price of Your gifts. May all forget sorrow, and the world get a new life in the splendour of a new sunrise of wisdom. Let those blind with hatred wake to a new sight of love.

Sorrowful is the heart of the earth. Man's heart is poisoned with material craving without shame. Countries far and wide put on with pride the blood-red mark of hatred.

Shower your grace on us, make us one in spirit, bringing harmony into our lives.

O Serene, O Free, in Your immeasurable mercy, wash out all dark stains from the heart of this earth.

Pardon Me, Too

Pardon me, too.
Give me, too, O Lord, the particle of nectar.
Leaving home, seated am I on the way.
Have thy feet on my heart as well.
Know I, a dirty son of thee am I –
At thy feet I, too, shall be given a refuge.
Myself in sin am I drowned, in mental agony am I weeping,
O listen to the pains of my heart as well.

Accept Me

Accept me, my Lord, accept me for a while and don't go back.

Let those orphaned days that passed without You be
forgotten.
May my life, held under Your light, be ever awake.

I have wandered here and there in pursuit of voices that
drew me, yet led me nowhere.

Now let me sit in peace and listen to Your words in the
soul of my silence.

Do not turn away Your face from my heart's dark secrets,
but burn them till they are alight and Your fire.

When the Heart is Hard

When the heart is hard and parched, come upon me with a shower of mercy.

When grace is lost from life, come with a burst of song.

When tumultuous work raises its din on all sides, shutting me out from beyond, come to me, God silence, with Your peace and rest.

When my beggarly heart sits crouched, shut up in a corner, break open the door, my God.

When desire blinds the mind with delusion and dust, O Holy One, come with Your light and Your thunder.

Rain

The day is dim with rain.

Angry lightning glances through the tattered cloud-veils, and the forest is like a caged lion shaking its mane in despair.

On such a day amid the winds beating their wings, let me find my peace in Your presence.

For the sorrowing sky has shadowed my solitude, to deepen the meaning of Your touch about my heart.

Let Me

Let me not pray to be sheltered from dangers but to be fearless in facing them.

Let me not beg for soothing my pain but for the heart to conquer it.

Let me not look for allies in life's battlefield, but rely on my own strength.

Let me not crave in anxious fear to be saved, but hope for the courage to win my freedom.

Let me not seek solace in Your lightening my burden but for the strength to bear it.

Grant me that I may not be a coward, feeling Your mercy in my success alone, but let me find the grasp of Your hand in my failure.

It is He

It is He, the innermost one, who awakens my being with His deep unseen touches.

It is He who puts His enchantments upon these eyes and joyfully plays on the chords of my heart in varied cadence of pleasure and pain.

It is He who weaves the web of this enchantment in evanescent hues of gold and silver, blue and green, and lets it peep out through the folds of his feet, at whose touch I forget myself.

Days come and ages pass, and it is ever He who moves my heart in many a name, in many a guise, in rapture of joy and sorrow.

Your Pleasure

You have made me endless, such is Your pleasure. This frail vessel You empty again and again and fill it ever with new life.

This little flute of a reed you have carried over hills and dales, and have breathed through it melodies eternally new.

At the immortal touch of Your hands my little heart loses its limits in joy and burst into expression ineffable.

Your endless gifts shower into these tiny hands of mine. Ages pass, and still You pour, and still there is room to fill.

Your Love

Let Your love play upon my voice and rest on my silence.

Let it pass through my heart into all my movements.

Let Your love, like stars, shine in the darkness of my sleep and dawn in my awakening.

Let it burn in the flame of my desires and flow in all currents of my own love.

Let me carry Your love in my life as a harp does its music, and give it back to You at last with my life.

Light

Light, my light, the world-filling light, the eye-kissing light, the heart-sweetening light:

Ah, the light dances, my Darling, at the centre of my life; the light strikes, my Darling, the chords of my love; the sky opens; the wind runs wild; laughter passes over the earth.

The butterflies spread their sails on the sea of light. Lilies and jasmine surge up on the crest of the waves of light.

The light is shattered into gold on very cloud, my darling, and it scatters gems in profusion.

Mirth spreads from leaf to leaf, my Darling, and gladness without measure. The heaven's river has drowned its banks, and the flood of joy is abroad.

The Fullness of Peace

Not for me is the love that knows no restraint and is like a foaming wine that, having burst its vessel in a moment, would run to waste.

Send me the love that is cool and pure like Your rain, which blesses the thirsty earth and fills the homely earthen jars.

Send me the love that would soak down into the centre of being, and from there would spread like the unseen sap through the branching tree of life, giving birth to fruits and flowers.

Send me the love that keeps the heart still with the fullness of peace.

Life of my Life

Life of my life, I shall ever try to keep my body pure, knowing that Your living touch is upon all my limbs.

I shall ever try to keep all untruths from my thoughts, knowing that You are that truth which has kindled the light of reason in my mind.

I shall ever try to drive all evils away from my heart and keep my love in flower, knowing that You have Your seat in the inmost shrine of my heart.

It shall be my endeavour to reveal You in my actions, knowing it is Your power that gives me strength to act.

Salutation

In one salutation to You, my God, let all my senses spread out and touch this world at Your feet.

Like a raincloud hung low with its burden of unshed showers, let all my mind bend down at Your door in one salutation to You.

Let all my songs gather together their diverse strains into a single current and flow to a sea of silence in one salutation to You.

Like a flock of homesick cranes flying night and day back to their mountain nests, let all my life take its voyage to its eternal home in one salutation to You.

You are There

I would leave this chanting and singing and telling of beads. Whom do I worship in this lonely dark corner of a temple with doors all shut? I open my eyes and see that, You, O God, are not before me.

You are there where the tiller is tilling the hard ground and where the pathmaker is breaking stones. You are with them in sun and in shower, and Your garment is covered with dust. I put off my holy mantle and even, like You, come down on the dusty soil.

Deliverance? Where is deliverance to be found? You Yourself have joyfully taken upon Yourself the bonds of creation; You are bound with us all forever.

I come out of my meditations and leave aside my flowers and incense. What harm if my clothes become tattered and stained? I meet You and stand by You in toil and in the sweat of my brow.

Leave your Burdens

O fool, to try to carry yourself upon your own shoulders! O beggar, to come to beg at your own door!

Leave all your burdens in His hands that can bear all, and never look behind in regret.

Your desire at once puts out the light from the lamp it touches with its breath. It is unholy – do not take your gifts from its unclean hands. Accept only what is offered by sacred love.

Seated am I at the Door

Seated am I, O Lord, at the door – tears roll down my eyes
O what is there in the world – the heart remains
     unfulfilled
Nursing the wishes of the heart have I wandered here
     from door to door
Leaving all have I come here, deprive not the poor
and ignored.
Do whatever you like but I shall remain beside thee.

Hold my Hand

Deliver me from my own shadows, O God, from the wreck and confusion of my days, for the night is dark and Your pilgrim is blinded.

Hold my hand.

Deliver me from despair.
Touch with Your flame the lightless lamp of my sorrow.
Waken my tired strength from its sleep.
Do not let me linger behind, counting my losses.
Let the road sing to me of the house at every step.
For the night is dark, and Your pilgrim is blinded.

Hold my hand.

Locked Heart

If ever the door to my heart be locked do not turn back, my Lord. Break it open and take Your place in the innermost shrine of my heart.

If ever the strings of my heart do not sing Your praise wait for a moment and do not turn back, my Lord.

If ever I do not answer Your call, wake me up with the pain of thunder and do not turn back, my Lord.

If I ever offer Your place to someone else, do not turn back, my eternal King of Kings.

Burdens

Light is the burdens You gave me to bear but heavy are those I gather myself. Do take them away, my Friend.

Rolling like a heavy stone I am, who knows where? Stop this running, my Friend, do stop it.

The fire of my sorrow, that I invite, turns my heart into cinder and nothing grows there. Sweet pains are your gifts, which heal my soul like showers soothe the parched earth.

Whatever I found I saved them all. Whoever sees them demand their price, showing no mercy at all.

Rolling like a stone I am. Stop this journey, my Friend, do stop it.

Your Presence

I know not from what distant time You are ever coming nearer to meet me.

Your sun and Your stars can not keep You hidden from me forever.

In many a morning and evening Your footsteps I have heard and Your messenger has come within my heart and called me in whisper.

O travelling comrade mine, I know not why today my life is astir and a feeling of tremulous joy is passing through my heart.

It is as if the time has come today to wind up my work, for I sense in the air a faint sweet smell of Your presence.

Treasures

I know that the day will come when my sight of this earth shall be lost, and life will take its leave in silence, drawing the last curtain over my eyes.

Yet stars will watch at night, and morning rise as before, and hours heave like sea waves casting up pleasures and pains.

When I think of this end of my moments, the barrier of the moments breaks, and I see by the light of death Your world with its careless treasures. Rare is its lowliest seat; rare is its meanest of lives.

Things that I longed for in vain and things that I got – let them pass. Let me but truly posses the things that I ever spurned and overlooked.

My Country

Let the earth and the water, the air and the fruits of my country be sweet, my God.

Let the homes and markets, the forests and the fields of my country be bountiful, my God.

Let the promises and hopes, the deeds and the words of my country be true, my God.

Let the lives and hearts of the sons and daughters of my country be one, my God.

With the Light of the New Sun

Remain in joy at all time in the world fearless and with a
    heart pure.
Awake in joy in the morning, work in joy,
in songs of joy return home in the evening.
Remain in goodness in crisis and affluence,
in disgrace and dishonour remain in joy.
In joy remain by pardoning all,
in drinking peace in the fountain of nectar for ever.

SONGS

Gitanjali 95

I was not aware of the moment when I first crossed the threshold of this life.

What was the power that made me open out into this vast mystery like a bud in the forest at midnight!

When in the morning I looked upon the light I felt in a moment that I was no stranger in this world, that the inscrutable without name and form had taken me in its arms in the form of my own mother.

Even so, in death the same unknown will appear as ever known to me. And because I love this life, I know I shall love death as well.

The child cries out when from the right breast the mother takes it away, in the very next moment to find in the left one its consolation.

Gitanjali 61

The sleep that flits on baby's eyes – does anybody know from where it comes? Yes, there is a rumour that it has its dwelling where, in the fairy village among shadows of the forest dimly lit with glow-worms, there hang two timid buds of enchantment. From there it comes to kiss baby's eyes.

The smile that flickers on baby's lips when he sleeps – does anybody know where it was born? Yes, there is a rumour that a young pale beam of a crescent moon touched the edge of a vanishing autumn cloud, and there the smile was first born in the dream of a dew-washed morning – the smile that flickers on baby's lips when he sleeps.

The sweet, soft freshness that blooms on baby's limbs – does anybody know where it was hidden so long? Yes, when the mother was a young girl it lay pervading her heart in tender and silent mystery of love – the sweet, soft freshness that has bloomed on baby's limbs.

Oh my Lord, oh my friend . . .

Oh my Lord, oh my friend,
night and day
you are close to me.
You are my joy
you are my peace
you are the sea of tranquillity
yours is the haven of happiness
calming our souls
removing sorrow.
All suffering ceases at your feet.

You,
the refuge
of all humanity.

Gitanjali 4

Life of my life, I shall ever try to keep my body pure, knowing that thy living touch is upon all my limbs.

I shall ever try to keep all untruths out from my thoughts, knowing that thou art that truth which has kindled the light of reason in my mind.

I shall ever try to drive all evils away from my heart and keep my love in flower, knowing that thou hast thy seat in the inmost shrine of my heart.

And it shall be my endeavour to reveal thee in my actions, knowing it is thy power gives me strength to act.

Gitanjali 69

The same stream of life that runs through my veins night and day runs through the world and dances in rhythmic measures.

It is the same life that shoots in joy through the dust of the earth in numberless blades of grass and breaks into tumultuous waves of leaves and flowers.

It is the same life that is rocked in the ocean-cradle of birth and of death, in ebb and in flow.

I feel my limbs are made glorious by the touch of this world of life. And my pride is from the life-throb of ages dancing in my blood this moment.

You were hidden in my heart . . .

You were hidden in my heart
but I did not see you,
I looked outwards,
not within myself.

In all my loves,
in all my hopes and hurts,
you were there beside me,
but I did not turn to you.

You filled with joy
every action of my life.
But in my happiness
I forgot you.

Enshrined deep within me,
your melody ran through
all my joys and sorrows,
but I failed
to sing to you.

Gitanjali 59

Yes, I know, this is nothing but thy love, O beloved of my heart – this golden light that dances upon the leaves, these idle clouds sailing across the sky, this passing breeze leaving its coolness upon my forehead.

The morning light has flooded in my eyes – this is thy message to my heart. Thy face is bent from above, thy eyes look down on my eyes, and my heart has touched thy feet.

Gitanjali 72

He it is, the innermost one, who awakens my being with his deep hidden touches.

He it is who puts his enchantment upon these eyes and joyfully plays on the chords of my heart in varied cadence of pleasure and pain.

He it is who weaves the web of this maya in evanescent hues of gold and silver, blue and green, and lets peep out through the folds his feet, at whose touch I forget myself.

Days come and ages pass, and it is ever he who moves my heart in many a name, in many a guise, in many a rapture of joy and of sorrow.

This path . . .

This path
on the red earth
meandering through the fields
has enchanted me.

My mind tries to reach out
Along the dusty road –
to whom?

My feet become restless
I long to go –
I do not know where.
What treasures are hidden
around the corner?
What surprises await me?

I go on dreaming –
where does it end?

Gitanjali 8

The child who is decked with prince's robes and who has jewelled chains round his neck loses all pleasure in his play; his dress hampers him at every step.

In fear that it may be frayed, or stained with dust he keeps himself from the world, and is afraid even to move.

Mother, it is no gain, thy bondage of finery, if it keep one shut off from the healthful dust of the earth, if it rob one of the right of entrance to the great fair of common human life.

In your infinity . . .

In your infinity
no matter how far I go
with my mind and soul,
I never encounter sorrow, death or separation.
Death reveals itself,
sorrow becomes a bottomless pit,
when I turn away from you
and see only myself.

O perfect one!
All that there is,
lies at your feet,
except fear –
It is mine only, and I cry day and night.

The turmoil of the soul,
the burden of life
all disappear with the blink of an eye,
when I see you enthroned in my life and heart.

Gitanjali 36

This is my prayer to thee, my lord — strike, strike at the root of penury in my heart.

Give me the strength lightly to bear my joys and sorrows.

Give me the strength to make my love fruitful in service.

Give me the strength never to disown the poor or bend my knees before insolent might.

Give me the strength to raise my mind high above daily trifles.

And give me the strength to surrender my strength to thy will with love.

I shall have to give you my all . . .

I shall have to give you my all,
I know –
all my treasures,
all my thoughts
all that I see with my eyes,
all that I hear.
The service of my hands,
all my comings and goings,
I have to give to you.
My mornings
my evenings
will blossom towards you.

In the seclusion of my heart
my veena is being strung now
to play to your tune
when the time comes.
The joys and sorrows that are mine
make them yours
with your love;
all that I have ever received
will truly become mine
when I give them to you.

Gitanjali 49

You came down from your throne and stood at my cottage door.

I was singing all alone in a corner, and the melody caught your ear. You came down and stood at my cottage door

Masters are many in your hall, and songs are sung there at all hours. But the simple carol of this novice struck at your love. One plaintive little strain mingled with the great music of the world, and with a flower for a prize you came down and stopped at my cottage door.

With your compassion . . .

With your compassion
my life
will have to be cleansed,
or else
how can I touch your feet?
When I bring my offering of prayers
to you,
my failings come in the way,
and my heart cannot reach you.

All this time
I was impervious to pain
being covered with impurities
of my own self.
Today my heart cries out in anguish,
I long for your sublime presence.
do not, oh do not
keep me lying in the dust
any more.

Gitanjali 57

Light, my light, the world-filling light, the eye-kissing light, heart-sweetening light!

Ah, the light dances, my darling, at the centre of my life; the light strikes, my darling, the chords of my love; the sky opens, the wind runs wild, laughter passes over the earth.

The butterflies spread their sails on the sea of light. Lilies and jasmines surge up on the crest of the waves of light.

The light is shattered into gold on every cloud, my darling, and it scatters gems in profusion.

Mirth spreads from leaf to leaf, my darling, and gladness without measure. The heaven's river has drowned its banks and the flood of joy is abroad.

Gitanjali 90

On the day when death will knock at thy door what wilt thou offer to him?

Oh, I will set before my guest the full vessel of my life – I will never let him go with empty hands.

All the sweet vintage of all my autumn days and summer nights, all the earnings and gleanings of my busy life will I place before him at the close of my days when death will knock at my door.

Protection from danger . . .

Protection from danger
is not what I ask from you.
Let me have the courage
to face it.

To be consoled in my sorrow
is not what I ask from you.
Let me have the strength
to conquer it.

Let me rely on my own self
when there is no one to support me.
Let me not lose faith in myself
when deception surrounds me.
I do not ask
for the lightening of my burden,
may I be able
to bear it.

In my days of joy
I shall see you before me.
In my days of sorrow and darkness
let me not doubt your presence
before me

Gitanjali 100

I dive down into the depth of the ocean of forms, hoping
to gain the perfect pearl of the formless.

No more sailing from harbour to harbour with this
my weather-beaten boat. The days are long passed when
my sport was to be tossed on waves.

And now I am eager to die into the deathless.

Into the audience hall by the fathomless abyss
where swells up the music of toneless strings I shall take
this harp of my life.

I shall tune it to the notes of forever, and when it
has sobbed out its last utterance, lay down my silent harp
at the feet of the silent.

It is time for me to go . . .

It is time for me to go –
but they keep calling me back.
The light of early dawn
peeping through the clouds
keeps calling me back.

The wistful songs of birds
from behind the foliage of the woods
keep calling me back.

The music of the river,
flowing on –
through shadowy glades,
in quest of what –
it does not know,
keeps calling me back.

On this morning of farewell,
someone within me
keeps calling me back.

Be happy . . .

Be happy
always –
Without fear,
with heart unblemished.
Be happy,
always –
With joy in life.

Let there be joy
when you awake in
the morning.
Let there be joy
when you labour through the day.
Let your gladness
when you rest in the evening,
Burst forth into joyful songs.

May each turn of fortune
bring its own fulfilment.
May your endurance enhance
with each voice of dissent.
Forgive all,
and be happy.
May peace descend on you
like nectar from heaven.
Be happy always,
with joy in life.

CONTEMPLATIONS

Thy sunshine smiles upon the winter days of my heart,
    never doubting of its spring flowers.

*

It is the tears of the earth that
keep her smiles in bloom.

Listen, my heart, the whispers of the world
with which it makes love to you.

*

What you are you do not see,
what you see is your shadow.

He has made his weapons his gods.
When his weapons win
he is defeated himself.

✳

The fish in the water is silent,
the animal on the earth is noisy,
the bird in the air is singing.

But man has in him the silence of the sea,
the noise of the earth
and the music of the air.

We come nearest to the great
when we are great in humility.

*

God grows weary of great kingdoms,
but never of little flowers.

The mist, like love, plays upon the heart of the hills
and brings out surprises of beauty.

*

Your voice, my friend, wanders in my heart,
like the muffled sound of the sea
among these listening pines.

This longing is for the one who is felt in the dark,
but not seen in the day.

*

Death's stamp gives value to the coin of life;
making it possible to buy with life
what is truly precious.

Do not linger to gather flowers to keep them,
but walk on, for flowers will keep themselves
blooming all your way.

✳

Be still, my heart, these great trees are prayers.

The bird thinks it is an act of kindness
to give the fish a lift in the air.

*

'In the moon thou sendest thy love letters to me,'
said the night to the sun.

'I leave my answers in tears upon the grass.'

If you shut your door to all errors truth will be shut out.

*

The roots below the earth claim no rewards
for making the branches fruitful.

Let me think that there is one among those stars
that guides my life through the dark unknown.

❋

Woman, with the grace of your fingers
you touched my things
and order came out like music.

Silence will carry your voice like the nest
that holds the sleeping birds.

When we rejoice in our fullness,
then we can part with our fruits with joy.

That which oppresses me,
is it my soul trying to come out in the open,
or the soul of the world knocking at my heart
for its entrance?

*

'Who drives me forward like fate?'
'The Myself striding on my back.'

They hated and killed and men praised them.

But God in shame hastens to hide its memory
under the green grass.

When the sun goes down to the West,
the East of his morning
stands before him in silence.

The stream of truth flows through its channels of mistakes.

❊

This life is the crossing of a sea,
where we meet in the same narrow ship.

In death we reach the shore
and go to our different worlds.

I come to your shore as a stranger,
I lived in your house as a guest,
I leave your door as a friend, my earth.

*

Light in my heart the evening star of rest
and then let the night whisper to me of love.

One word keep for me in thy silence, O World,
when I am dead, 'I have loved.'

*

While I was passing with the crowd in the road
I saw thy smile from the balcony
and I sang and forgot all noise.

When all the strings of my life will be tuned, my Master,
then at every touch of thine will come out the music of love.

*

Clouds come floating into my life from other days
no longer to shed rain or usher storm
but to give colour to my sunset sky.

Blessed is he whose fame does not outshine his truth.

*

Tonight there is a stir among the palm leaves; a swell
in the sea, Full moon, like the heart throb of the world.
From what unknown sky hast thou carried
in thy silence the aching secret of love?

The smell of the wet earth in the rain rises like a great chant of praise from the voiceless multitude of the insignificant.

*

We shall know some day that death can never rob us of that which our soul has gained, for her gains are one with herself.

I have scaled the peak and found no shelter
in fame's bleak and barren height. Lead me,
my Guide, before the light fades, into the valley of
quiet where life's harvest mellows into golden wisdom.

*

When you give yourself truly and fully
You encounter an image of beauty.

The plough cuts the earth for its fruit.
From the scratches of pen on paper
come the produce of mind and heart.

The stamp of Death
    gives value to living;
    hence in our giving
of life, there is worth.

Where feeling is lacking,
            spikes are all you get:
plants in the desert
            are thorny and squat.

*

If you want to be bigger than you are,
    to your own self humbly bow.

When a man treats love as a business proposition,
love takes a backseat view of the action.

*

Work is our duty, that's quite true.
But shame on those who only think
of work they must do.

I thought I knew you in my heart, my love,
    but maybe I did not.
You kept some things to yourself, because
    your feelings were hurt.

*

Let lightless, hopeless, merciless outer pain
be healed by the limitless light that shines within!

Like a lotus of light, the setting sun
    has closed its petals up.
    Let it bloom in a new tongue,
    with new unfaltering hope,
    on the shore of a new dawn!

✳

Let my love, in my work by day, find energy;
then, in the night, find deep peace and harmony.

Let go of what must go!
It will cause you hurt
if you do not open the door
to let it out.

*

Why do our thoughts keep dwelling on future fruits?
Let flowers on the branch suffice to gladden our hearts!

The perfect player looks for an instrument that will suit.
　　The player, meanwhile, is sought by a perfect flute.

*

When the sky is grey,
　　the grieving clouds forget
that they themselves
　　have blotted the sunshine out.

The mist may seem to throw the mountain into obscurity,
but nothing can shake its grand, unmoving majesty!

*

A moth counts not by years,
but moment by moment:
so the time it has is sufficient.

✳

I slept and dreamt that life was joy. I awoke and saw
that life was service. I acted and behold, service was joy.

✳

Sources

We are grateful to the following for permission to reproduce material from their editions of Rabindranath Tagore's writings.

Prose

Extracts are taken from *Lectures & Addresses by Rabindranath Tagore*, selected by Anthony X. Soares (1928, Macmillan and Co. Ltd, London), with kind permission of the Chancellor, Rabindra Bhavana, Visva-Bharati University, Santiniketan.

Poems

New Birth; Recovery – 14; Question; The Borderland – 9

from *Rabindranath Tagore: Selected Poems*, translated by William Radice (1985, Penguin Books, London, UK).

Life; On my Birthday; Not my Achievement; The Introduction; The Impermanence; Vitality; Sister; Deliverance; The Riddle; Infinite Love; The Look; First Kiss; Two Women; The Prisoner; Alone; The End; The Beacon; The Final Offering; Farewell; A Hundred Years from Today / 1996.

from *Poems of Rabindranath Tagore*, edited by Humayun Kabir, (2005, UBS Publishers, Distributors Pvt. Ltd in association with Visva-Bharati University, Santiniketan, India).

Prayers

The World Gone Mad; Accept Me; Let Me; It is He; Your Pleasure; Leave your Burdens; Locked Heart; Burdens; My Country

from *Prayers from the Heart*, Rabindranath Tagore, edited & translated by Jadu Saha (2009, Shipra Publications, Delhi, India).

When the Heart is Hard; Rain; Your Love; Light; The Fullness of Peace; Life of my Life; Salutation; You are There; Hold my Hand; Your Presence; Treasures

from *The Heart of God*, Prayers of Rabindranath Tagore, selected & edited by Herbert F. Vetter (1997, Tuttle Publishing, Vermont, USA).

Oh Make Me Thy Servant; Pardon Me, Too; Seated am I at the Door; With the Light of the New Sun

from *Rabindranath Tagore Songs of Prayer*, Mohit Chakrabarti (2006, New Age Books, Delhi, India).

Songs

Oh my lord, oh my friend . . . , You were hidden in my heart . . . , This path . . . , In your infinity . . . , I shall have to give you my all . . . , With your compassion . . . , Protection from danger . . . , It is time for me to go . . . , Be happy . . .

from *Some Poems & Songs of Tagore*, translated by Sovana Dasgupta (2004, Rupa & Co., Delhi, India).

Songs from the *Gitanjali* are from the 2006 edition, Full Circle Publishing, Delhi, India.

Contemplations

Those on pages 121 to 140 (top) are from *Stray Birds* by Tagore (www.readbookonline.net/readOnLine/1007).

Those on pages 140 (bottom) to 148 are from *Rabindranath Tagore, Particles, Jottings, Sparks: The Collected Brief Poems*, translated with an introduction by William Radice (2001, Angel Books, London, UK).

FOURTEEN SONGS
by Rabindranath Tagore

learned, translated and introduced
at the Bard's wish
by Arthur Geddes

Foreword by Jawarhal Nehru

This songbook contains fourteen of Tagore's songs that were translated from Bengali by Arthur Geddes. From 1921 to 1924 Geddes was in India assisting the town-planning work of his father Patrick Geddes and also the rural reconstruction projects of Tagore at Sriniketan. It was during this period that he learned Bengali, sang and made notations of some of Tagore's songs and played the melodies on his violin. He greatly admired Rabindranath Tagore, and continued to share and raise awareness of Tagore's poems and songs at home and abroad.

There are five songs from 'Raja, the King of the Dark Chamber'; seven songs of prayer, resolution and mourning; and two songs of youth and Santiniketan.

Published by Resurgence Books and distributed by Green Books
ISBN 978 0 85784 022 6
40pp large format paperback £12.95

For our full list of books see www.greenbooks.co.uk